How Did God Create Humankind?
Scientific and Biblical Views

*From the chaos of evolution to the mystery
of faith and redemption*

Dr. Ali Ansarifar

Dr. Ali Ansarifar

Kingdom Publishers

www.kingdompublishers.co.uk

How Did God Create Humankind?
Scientific and biblical views

Copyright© Dr Ali Ansarifar

All rights reserved. No part of this book may be reproduced in any form by photocopying or any electronic or mechanical means, including information storage or retrieval systems, without permission in writing from both the copyright owner and the publisher of the book. The right of to be identified as the author of this work has been asserted by him in accordance with the Copyright, Designs and Patents Act 1988 and any subsequent amendments thereto. A catalogue record for this book is available from the British Library.

All scripture quotations have been taken from The Interlinear Bible, Hebrew- Greek- English. Jay P. Green, Sr. Hendrickson Publishers

ISBN: 978-1-911697-64-0

1st Edition by Kingdom Publishers
Kingdom Publishers
London, UK.

You can purchase copies of this book from any leading bookstore or email contact@kingdompublishers.co.uk

Dr. Ali Ansarifar

The conflict between science and religion has roots in the past and persists even today. Science is based on empirical observations supported by mathematics, whereas religion is based on a rich history of human beliefs, belief systems, and experiences. In religion, ideas, teachings, and historical events are accepted by faith, often without proof. In empirical science, however, proof results from a carefully considered hypothesis, theory, or observation, meticulously designed and executed experiments, and a detailed analysis of the results, often supported by mathematics. It seems that these two disciplines can never be consolidated. But, science does not prove or disprove the existence of a supernatural God, and therefore, scientific knowledge may be used to understand the biblical account of creation. Science tells us that the universe, celestial bodies, and life on earth resulted from a random Big Bang event in the distant past. That life evolved over millions of years through the struggle for existence by natural selection and has no purpose. The book of Genesis is a chronological account of the creation of the universe and life on Earth. It does not address how God did it, but science explains how it all happened. When the stated purpose of redeeming humanity in the Bible is combined with scientific knowledge, it produces a fascinating story to tell. It is doubtful that human wisdom will ever understand the marvels of God's creation and its intricate workings and find answers to all the questions. Still, for now, we can have an understanding based on scientific knowledge and biblical revelation and can do no more or any better.

Dedication

To those who serve the greatest servant of all time, Jesus Christ, and strive to improve humanity and make the world a better place to live in.
-Pastor Martin Mitchell

Disclaimer

It has never been the intention of the author of this book to infringe on the sensitivity, personal faith, and belief of his readers. The material and information presented in this book are never meant to cause offence to any individual person or group of people of any race, nationality, creed, and background. This book is written for educational purposes and academic interest only.

It is incredible that flesh comes into being from the light and inhabits material poverty. It is also remarkable that flesh has an inner heart that seeks after its Creator, the light. It is even more astounding that Jesus Christ redeems the inner soul of mortal man, changing it into pure light for perpetuity. It is the wonder of all wonders that righteousness comes into existence from mortal flesh despite such immense darkness and adversity. For a mortal, righteousness is the path to salvation and eternal life.

A call to share the gospel with others is a privilege granted to a few who are called to serve Jesus Christ for the glory of God and redemption of humanity.

A perfect being can never be created instantly since a being comes into existence of its own accord. And when it does, it can thenceforth be made perfect like Jesus Christ by the Holy God.

Anybody who finds the truth in the Bible wonders why human beings' innocence, self-worth, dignity, and self-respect are violated so belligerently for so long. By God's grace and mercy, all that is noble and righteous in human nature will be changed into a perfect oneness in Jesus Christ for eternity. But first, repentance must come.

A farmer plants wheat seeds on his farm and waters the soil until wheat grows. But, to his bitter disappointment, the harvest produced little wheat and many weeds. How sad that so much farmland is squandered for the sake of a few grains of wheat.

The seed was good, but the soil was infertile and the harvest poor. How can the harvest be blamed for the soil's infertility and the sower's mentality?

A farmer harvests his grains of wheat and makes them into flour. He gives the flour to a baker who mixes it with water to make a dough. The baker then uses the dough to make a loaf of bread and alms it to the hungry. The hungry eat the bread and say, "Blessed is the baker who made the bread, and hallowed be the farmer who sowed the wheat, for he knew of my hunger."

The Holy God sowed a redeemer in the womb of the Virgin Mary. The redeemer became incarnate in Jesus Christ, healed the sick, consoled the bereaved, forgave sinners, raised hope for the oppressed, converted the pagan, and resurrected the dead. The righteous cry, "Blessed is the womb that gave birth to my redeemer, and hallowed be the Father who bestows mercy and rest on my soul."

The Cross of mercy

Redemption rests with the Cross, and damnation is with the sword.
Whoever has mercy through the Cross will live despite the sword.
But whoever has no hope in the Cross will perish by the sword.

The sword of judgement

"Crucify him," the crowd shouted. The Cross of Calvary became a sword of destruction for all. For those in the east, the west, the north, and the south, the sword brought immense suffering and death. Reprisal is falling on the sword-bearer, and one wonders for whom the bell is tolling.

We come from the hell of mass extinctions, natural disasters, asteroid impacts, epidemics of disease, famine, injustice, and tribal, regional, and global warfare and bloodshed, and we are going to the hell of judgement and damnation. But, how wise are those who trust Jesus Christ to get them out of this mayhem and darkness and bring them to the light of the Father.

Contents

Chapter 1
A cosmological model of the Universe –
The Big Bang theory and space — 31

Chapter 2
The struggle for life by means of natural selection –
Millennia of mayhem. — 41

Chapter 3
Biblical and cosmological views of the origin
of all things – the universe and humankind — 49

Chapter 4
The scientific view of the origin of humankind — 59

Chapter 5
A scientific/biblical view of the origin of God
and creation of humankind — 67

Chapter 6
The greatest mystery of all – Faith, redemption,
and the kingdom of light — 77

Chapter 7
Summary and conclusions — 89
References — 93
Epilogue — 95
Afterword — 97
Final remarks — 99
About the author — 101
About the book — 103

Chapter 1
A cosmological model of the Universe – The Big Bang theory and space

In a cosmological model of the universe, there is no place for an omnipotent and omniscient Holy God. The galaxies and all living beings are the by-products of a major random event in the past named the Big Bang. Since the laws of physics that govern the universe are absolute, a creator inside the universe or outside it has no freedom to intervene to change them arbitrarily. Our universe will eventually decay and re-collapse inward to a point from which it and our existence come. In the final collapse, all the matter and light will vanish, and the universe will become cold, lifeless, and dark.

The Western European Enlightenment during the 17th and 18th centuries, referred to as the Age of Reason, led to major advances in our understanding of the origin of the universe and life on earth. The rise of modern empirical science such as physics and astronomy, coupled with mathematics, and the invention of the microscope, telescope, thermometer, and pendulum clock opened our eyes to the complexity, mysteries, and beauty of the cosmos. [1] The laws of physics and biology completely explain the origin and evolution of the universe and life on earth, leaving no room for a creation and a creator. In this chapter, the cosmological model will be examined briefly.

The Big Bang - Like many great ideas and discoveries in the history of science, the origin of the Big Bang theory has its own fascinating story. The general theory of relativity that was proposed by Albert Einstein is a theory of space and time as well as a new theory of gravity. It explains how objects move through the universe and how the universe itself evolves. In the early years, as far back as 1917, the universe was considered to be static and eternal. The Milky Way galaxy was the only one surrounded by vast, infinite, dark, and empty space. Gravity is a purely attractive force between all objects, so it is impossible to have a set of masses located in space at rest forever. The masses collapse inward because of their mutual gravitational attraction. This contradicted the static universe and had to be abandoned. The expanding universe began as an infinitesimal point, which is called the "Primeval Atom", in an incredibly hot, dense Big Bang roughly 13.72 billion years ago and has been expanding ever since. Since the universe had a beginning, it implies a creation. The Milky Way galaxy is one of perhaps 400 billion galaxies in the observable universe. Some years after the discovery of our expanding universe, the notion of a Big Bang is supported by independent empirical confirmation. Along with matter, there burst forth from nothing a sea of light and radiation, and the elements split and stirred and formed into millions of galaxies. The Big Bang may suggest a creator, but the mathematics of general relativity explains the evolution of the universe right back to its beginning without the intervention of any deity. [2] If the latter is true, then a creator is the effect or product of the Big Bang and not its cause. When the picture of the Big Bang (primeval fireball) is extrapolated to a time when the universe was about 1 second old, all observed matter was compressed in a dense plasma at a temperature of 10 billion degrees on the Kelvin scale. At this temperature, protons and neutrons react together as they bind together and then break apart from more collisions. Protons and neutrons are made of particles known as quarks. As the universe cools down, these particles bind to form different quantities of the nuclei of hydrogen, deuterium, helium, and lithium. The nucleus of lithium was the last to be formed during the Big Bang. The heavier nuclei, for example, nitrogen, iron, oxygen, and carbon, were not made in the Big Bang. They formed in the cores of stars that exploded into the cosmos and then merged with and around the earth to form us and everything else. So, the Big Bang had to be extremely hot to produce the abundance of light elements such as helium and lithium to ensure the expansion of the universe observed now. [2] In the subsequent years, science discovered antiparticles for almost every elementary particle in nature. Protons have antiprotons, and similarly, neutrons have antiparticles. Antiparticles have the same properties as particles, and when they meet, they annihilate into pure radiation, and we are back to square one, with no matter existing. For instance, electron-positron pairs can appear suddenly from nothing for a short time and then annihilate each other again. This gave rise to the notion of matter and antimatter in physics. The universe in which we live is made up of matter and has no antimatter. If the quantities of matter and antimatter were equal, no universe would have existed. [2]

Space - One of the most interesting discoveries of modern science is the nature of space. In essence, the universe came about from nothing. A simple version of nothing includes empty space, with nothing in it at all, and the laws of physics also existing. Empty space is very big and has energy even in the absence of any matter or radiation. In fact, enough energy to dominate the expansion of the universe. On very small scales, for very short times, empty space can appear to be a boiling and bubbling mix of virtual particles and fields fluctuating in magnitude and invisible on large scale. The small fluctuations in the density of matter and radiation that are caused during inflation result in the gravitational collapse of matter into galaxies and many other things we see today in the universe including us. The galaxies first formed about one billion years after the Big Bang. In fact, in the very early universe, the universe went through an inflationary period where space expanded and as it did so, it carried distant objects which were at rest in the space where they were resting, apart from one another at massive speeds. Before the inflation happened, everything within the observable universe was contained in a small region. When inflation ended, the energy stored in empty space turned into an energy of real particles and radiation, producing our present Big Bang expansion. Furthermore, about 99 percent of the universe that is made of dark matter and dark energy is invisible to humans. So, it seems we are the result of the small random quantum fluctuations in the density of matter and radiation during inflation that resulted from nothingness, and not a product of a creation by an omnipotent and omniscient God. [2] Quantum means the smallest amount or unit of some physical property, such as energy, that a system can possess. [3]

As mentioned earlier, empty space can have energy and expand very rapidly, so that the smallest regions could quickly reach a size to accommodate the entire visible universe. Therefore, the universe can start out as a small empty region of space and grow to huge sizes, containing a lot of radiation and matter. Inflation shows how empty space with energy can create everything we see along with a large and flat universe. So, space exists and can store energy, and using the laws of physics one can calculate the consequences. Therefore, the idea of ex nihilo creation has no scientific basis. Empty space is a boiling brew of virtual particles that pop in and out of existence in very short times. Particle-antiparticle pair nucleates out of empty space due to quantum fluctuation in a region. If the early universe began with equal amounts of matter and antimatter, all particles of matter and antimatter would have annihilated each other and there would be no matter left to make the galaxies, only emptiness, a radiation bath, and dark universe. It is also possible that there were equal amounts of matter and antimatter in an early hot, dense Big Bang, with a slight excess of matter over antimatter due to what is known as asymmetry or unevenness in the early universe. The small excess of matter would have had no comparable amount of antimatter to destroy it and hence there was no complete matter-antimatter annihilation, leading to nothing but pure radiation, and would be leftover, making up stars and galaxies we see today in the universe. [2]

There is also a possibility that many different universes might have risen, and the idea of universe does not necessarily mean everything that exists. The idea of a multiverse has gained considerable interest now. When the laws of physics as we understand them on small scales, are extended into a more complete theory, they suggest that our universe is one of many in existence and there is nothing special about our universe. In fact, we are the by-products of the complex laws governing the universe. Our universe comes into existence, develops, and evolves because these laws themselves require it to do so. This further weakens the need for a creation and a creator. Since the laws that govern the universe are absolute, a creator has no freedom to intervene to arbitrarily change them to do a supernatural act (a miracle) such as opening a sea for people to cross on a dry ground or changing the orbits of the celestial objects. [2]

In the inflationary picture, a huge energy temporarily dominates some region of the universe. This region begins to expand exponentially (rapidly perhaps a fraction of a second) and two possible events can happen. The quantum fluctuation during inflation may push the field that derives inflation to its lowest energy state, or in some regions, quantum fluctuations will drive the field toward yet higher energies. If the latter takes place, the inflation will continue for a longer time and more space will inflate. In these regions, quantum fluctuation will either cause some sub-regions to exit inflation and stop expanding rapidly, or there may be regions where quantum fluctuation will cause inflation to continue for much longer. This picture is called "chaotic inflation". In this model, some regions of space, will continue inflating forever. Those regions that leave inflation will become separate, and form disconnected universes or a multiverse. According to complex mathematics, it has been argued that a universe like ours must eventually decay and then re-collapse inward to a point, returning to the quantum cloud from which it and our existence came from. The universe will then disappear as abruptly as it began with all the matter and light vanishing, and the place becoming cold, lifeless, and dark. [2] So even light ends in this universe of ours.

Summary – As this brief review has shown, the cosmological model of the universe does not permit creation and a creator. The laws of physics govern the structure and behaviour of our universe from the beginning to the end, and no intervention in the working of the universe by a supernatural being is possible or permitted. There is no purpose for the universe and life on earth to exist. It is all a big accident, albeit a complex and magnificent one. This poses a major challenge to the traditional Judo-Christian account of the creation in Genesis in the Bible, which claims God created the universe. As Bible believers, we must meet this challenge.

Chapter 2
The struggle for life by means of natural selection – Millennia of mayhem.

Humanity has always marvelled at the beauty and complexities of the natural world. The vast number of organisms that are populating this plant is truly awe-inspiring. However, the processes that have produced life on earth are very destructive and ruthless. Natural selection dictates that only the healthy and fit species emerge from this mayhem of destruction to multiply and inhabit their habitations. Unfortunately, there is no room for a loving and caring creator in this gruesome struggle for life.

Charles Darwin (1809-1882) was one of the most influential thinkers of the 19th century. His book on the origin of species by means of natural selection or the preservation of favoured races in the struggle for life (originally published in 1859) was revolutionary in its content. It opened a new understanding of the natural world. The main components of Darwin's theory are the struggle for existence and natural selection, which will be discussed in this chapter briefly.

The struggle for existence and natural selection - Darwin explained how varieties are ultimately converted into good and distinct species. Distinct species differ from each other more than the varieties of the same species do. How do those groups of species, which constitute distinct genera, differ from each other more than the species of the same genus do? All these, he argued, result from the struggle for life. Any variation, no matter how minor and resulting from whatever cause, can benefit any individual of any species. In a highly complex relationship with other organic beings and with external nature, it will preserve that individual and will be passed on to its offspring. The offspring will also have a better chance of surviving since of the many individuals of any species that are periodically born; only a small number can survive. Darwin called the principle by which each slight variation, if useful, is preserved by the term Natural Selection. In nature, all organic beings are exposed to severe competition. The struggle for life in the natural world happens in different ways. Darwin's observation of the beauty of nature is alarming. He commented that there is often a superabundance of food. Still, we do not see that the birds singing around us mostly live on insects or seeds and are constantly destroying life, or their eggs, or their nestlings, are destroyed by birds and beasts of prey. Organic beings tend to increase at a high rate. Every bird and plant that produces several eggs or seeds must be destroyed at some point in its life, during certain seasons or years, to ensure that its population does not become so large that it can no longer support itself. If more individuals are produced than can possibly survive, there must be a struggle for existence either between one individual and another of the same species or between individuals of distinct species. The physical condition of life can also add to the struggle for existence. Every organic being strives to increase in numbers, and at some period during its life, it faces a struggle. Destruction may fall on the young or old during each generation or at a recurrent interval. When the level of destruction is reduced, the number of species increases. What exactly causes the natural tendency of each species to grow is not well understood. The nature of destruction varies from one species to another. For example, there is a vast destruction of seeds with plants, but seedlings suffer even worse from germinating in ground already thickly covered with other plants and from slugs and insects. [4] Many factors such as the amount of food for each species determine the extreme limit to which species can grow in number in the natural environment. Interestingly, it is not the obtaining food but the serving as prey to other animals which regulates the average number of species. Climate also plays a significant role in determining the average numbers of species, with periodical seasons of extreme, cold or drought being the most effective of all checks. Climate reduces food and causes the most intense struggle between individuals of the same species or of different species which relies on the same kind of food. At some period of its life, each species, suffers from enemies or competitors for the same place and food. This is made worse when climatic changes favour the enemies and competitors and increase their numbers, fully stocking each area with inhabitants, and the other species will diminish. Even when a species grows exceedingly in number due to favourable circumstances, in a small space, epidemics follow. Epidemics act as a limiting check on the species, independent of the struggle for life. Darwin stated that a plant could exist only where the conditions were so favourable that many could live together and thus save each other from utter destruction. [4] Darwin's observation of how one species determines the existence of other species is fascinating. In several parts of the world, insects determine the existence of cattle. For example, in some parts of the world, flies lay their eggs in the navels of cattle, horses, and dogs when first born. The increase of these flies must be checked by some means, e.g., by birds. Therefore, if certain insectivorous birds, whose numbers are regulated by other birds of prey, were to increase, the flies would decrease, and then cattle and horses would become wild and this would alter the vegetation, which in turn would affect the insects. So, this produces a highly complex set of independencies. The face of the natural world appears uniform over long periods, but this is deceiving. The struggle for life gives the victory to one organic being over another. Many different checks act on every species at different periods of life, seasons, or years to determine the average number or existence of the species. The plants and bushes that cloth an entangled bank exhibit beautiful diversity. However, this is the outcome of a struggle between the several kinds of trees during long centuries, the war between insect and insect, between insects, snails, and other animals with birds and beasts of prey, all trying to increase, and all feeding on each other or on the trees or their seeds and seedlings, and on the other plants which first appeared on the ground to check the growth of the trees. The struggle is most severe between the individuals of the same species that share the same districts, require the same food, and are exposed to the same dangers. [4]

In natural selection, individuals with an advantage over others have the best chance of surviving and procreating their kind. According to Darwin, any least harmful variation is destroyed, and natural selection is the preservation of favourable variations and the rejection of injurious ones. A change in the conditions of life acting on the reproduction system causes or increases variability. This is favourable to natural selection because profitable variations may occur, without which natural selection cannot be beneficial to organisms. Natural selection works if there are no negative variations and more positive ones. Therefore, natural selection is the gatekeeper of the natural world. It continuously scrutinises every variation in nature, rejecting the bad ones, preserving and adding up all that is good, and improving the condition of life for each organic being and its offspring. Natural selection acts by holding and accumulating infinitesimally minor inherited modifications, each useful to the organism. [4]

Summary - Darwin concluded that each organic being is attempting to increase in number at some period of its life. During some seasons of the year, they must struggle for life and suffer massive destruction during each generation or at intervals. No fear is felt in this struggle for existence, and the descent is quick. Only the healthy and fit species emerge from this mayhem of competition and death to multiply and populate their habitations. Natural selection is the maker of the natural world we see around us, and it will stop on its track without favourable variations, bringing organisms on earth to an end. Darwin removed the need for divine intervention in the evolution of life on earth. [4]

Chapter 3
Biblical and cosmological views of the origin of all things – the universe and humankind

The origin of God and the universe has always puzzled humankind. Our ancestors gazed at the heavens with awe and delighted in the wonders of the natural world but had no idea where they came from or how they were made. Since the Western European Enlightenment, advances in science and the invention of scientific instruments for observation and measurements have helped answer some of the questions. Still, the mysteries of the universe are not yet fully grasped. The two scientific premises, namely, quantum mechanics and the laws of physics, are at the forefront of our search for answers. The former premise is by far the most useful one in explaining the origin of God and the biblical account of the world's creation.

Biblical origin of God – The Bible contains verses about God and frequent references to light. "Have you not known? Have you not heard? Jehovah, the everlasting God, the creator of the ends of the earth; He is not faint, nor grows weary; there is no searching to His understanding." (Isaiah 40:28) "God is a spirit, and the ones worshipping

Him must worship in spirit and truth." (John 4:24) "And this is the message which we have heard from Him, and we announce to you: God is light, and no darkness is in Him – None." (1John 5). Jesus said, "If they say to you, 'Where are you from?' say to them, 'It is from the light that we have come – from the place where light, of its own accord alone, came into existence and stood at rest. And it has been shown forth in their image. If they say to you, "Is it you?" Say, 'We are its offspring, and we are chosen of the living father.' If they ask you, 'What is the sign of your father within you? Say to them, 'It is movement and repose.'" [5] (Thomas 50) The verses in the Bible do not reveal the origin of God, but there are references to Him as a spirit and light with no darkness in Him. But in Thomas 50, light (God) came into existence of its own accord and rested. We, humans, His children, are also made of light, giving us activity and rest. So, there is a place where God came into existence and had a beginning, but He was not created. It is left to us to speculate on the origin of God. Since God is light, and light and matter are the by-products of the Big Bang, the cosmological model may provide an answer.

Cosmological origin of God – The Big Bang, as previously stated, was caused by quantum fluctuations-induced inflation. [2] There are two possible explanations for the origin of light. a) Light appeared because of quantum fluctuations and became a conscious being like humans, whom we know as God. Then, God created the universe through the Big Bang. The reason that God created the universe is explained in the book "Why Did God Create Mankind?". [6] For this to happen, the universe was created with enough light, energy, and matter to enable God to create all the celestial bodies and life on earth. Hence, God had to precisely influence the quantum fluctuations-induced inflation (Big Bang) to create the universe he desired. In this scenario, God is outside the universe. b) A Big Bang created the universe, and light and matter were by-products of that. The light became a living being like humans and used the matter that was available to create the heavenly bodies and life on earth for the reasons explained in [6]. In this case, God is in the universe. Which scenario is more probable or even possible is not apparent, but let's consider the former for the sake of argument.

The light appeared because of quantum fluctuations and became a conscious being like humans, His children. But is the light solitude? "Light and darkness, life and death, right and left, are siblings (that are mutually dependent); it is impossible for them to separate. Accordingly, the good are not good, the bad are not bad, life is not life, and death is not death. So, each will be dispersed to its original source. But things that are superior to the world are indissoluble: they are eternal." [5] (Philip 6) Light and darkness coexisted from the beginning. But which one came first? According to Jesus, the light came into existence of its own accord and stood at rest. [5] So, the light had to come from somewhere, and darkness is the place where light (God) emerged from of its own accord. God was not created but had a beginning. The Judo-Christian picture of God as an old man with a long white beard creating the universe by some magical act at the tip of His finger is fanciful. The quantum fluctuations produced light, which is a living being. This being is known to us as God, Jehovah, Elohim, and many other names. But how can light be a conscious being? We are conscious beings made of matter. Matter is made of atoms, and atoms are light. [7] God is also a conscious being who lives and thinks like we do (Genesis 1:27). God does not have darkness in Him, and light and darkness remain fundamentally independent entities and oppose each other. But darkness and light coexist and cohabit in the place where the light came into existence of its own accord. About 99% of the universe is made of dark matter or dark energy, and only 1% is light, [2], causing duality, which had to be addressed because light could not have stayed in such immense darkness forever. Since light cannot destroy darkness from which it originates, physical separation between the two was the only option. The light was wise and devised a plan. It created the universe to free itself from coexisting with darkness in the same place. For all perpetuity, God separated light and darkness in the person of Jesus Christ and prepared the way for the dissolution of the duality of light and darkness. [6]

The cosmological model of the universe has no place for a creator. The laws of physics govern the structure and behaviour of our universe from the beginning to the end, and no intervention in the working of the universe by a supernatural being is possible or permitted. The universe is an accident and a by-product of the Big Bang, with no purpose for its existence. [2] Let us address this fault in the cosmological model using examples.

A universe with no purpose - Consider a household where a person X lives. This person is a teacher and must take a train to get to his workplace daily. He must use beds, a bathroom, and a kitchen in the house to get ready for work. He wakes up, washes, eats breakfast, dresses appropriately for his job, and leaves the house. He catches a taxi to the train station, buys a ticket, gets on the train to his destination, gets off at a station, and walks along the street to get to the school where he teaches. The routine has three stages: preparation for the journey at home, a highly structured Journey to work, and a clear purpose, to do a specific task. The journey was structured carefully from the start to the end, and the preparations at home were made for the occasion. If this person were to meet a friend for a social gathering, he would have prepared differently. For example, he would have chosen a different outfit, taken a different structured journey, and arrived at another destination. If there is no purpose, no journey will ever be taken, and no preparations will ever be made at home. So, the purpose drives the structure of the journey and all the preparations at home. No person can wake up in the morning and expect a random set of events at home to take him on an unplanned journey to a place where he may or may not perform a task; he may or may not know what that task is or is not. A well-defined purpose decides the journey's structure and preparations at home.

Now consider a person Y, who lives in the same house as person X. This person is an international travel salesman and must go to Germany for a meeting. He wakes up early in the morning by an alarm clock, washes, has breakfast, packs his suitcase, dresses up appropriately for the occasion, and leaves the house to get into a taxi to start his journey to the airport. The taxi travels on a well-planned route to the airport, where he disembarks, arrives at the departure terminal, and leaves for Germany. He arrives in Germany, takes a taxi to the hotel where the meeting takes place, and gives a presentation. The travel plan and the preparations that this person makes before the journey starts differs from those of person X, but they both live in the same house and use the same facilities. The same provisions at the source helped the two people to take journeys for entirely different reasons.

The conditions prevalent at the Big Bang could likely have produced a different universe depending on the reason for which it was created. Therefore, our universe is one of many universes that could have emerged from the Big Bang. Nevertheless, our universe is here, and no other universes are, as far as we know, because it has a specific purpose. Hence, we may contemplate a creator because of the necessity of purpose.

A universe with purpose - Let us apply this analogy to the universe. Since humanity started to study the celestial structures in the heavens and the living organisms on earth, it has been understood that strict laws of physics and biology have made them. As a result, we have been able to extrapolate back to the beginning of time when the initial conditions in the early universe were favourable for it to come into existence. We have been able to take a journey back to the beginning of time because we understand the laws of physics and biology that govern our universe and life on earth. Of course, this is a perfect science. But to argue from the Big Bang to the present day, we must accept that there must be a purpose for our universe to exist. We can no longer claim that after the Big Bang, the laws of physics and biology emerged as the universe cooled, and life appeared on Earth by chance and without reason or purpose.

Summary - We may now contemplate a creator God (light) and a purpose for the creation of the universe as this is the best we can do considering our incomplete knowledge of the cosmos and our ignorance of its exact origin. All indications are that quantum mechanics and the laws of physics and biology may be the best tools available for understanding the origin of God, the creation and evolution of the celestial bodies in the heavens and the organisms on earth.

In the next chapter, some scientific ideas about the origin of life on earth will be reviewed. However, the main interest will be in the origin and evolution of humankind.

Chapter 4
The scientific view of the origin of humankind

The evolution of life over millennia has produced the most colourful and unique variety of organisms we see on earth today. Science has made significant advances in understanding the origin of life, and the evolution of species is at the heart of this endeavour. According to science, humans have evolved from primitive apes, and there have been coexisting species of human ancestors throughout most of the evolutionary past that became extinct, paving the way for modern humans to emerge. The evolutionary path is littered with the death and destruction of countless other species along the way. Nevertheless, humanity seems to have emerged from the chaos of conflict, suffering, and extinction.

I believe and know that God loves to surprise and bless us and it's often in ways we never expect!

The primitive earth and the origin of life – The history of primitive earth is truly fascinating. Like other planets in the solar system, the Earth condensed out of a swirling cloud of gas surrounding the primitive sun and is estimated to be 4.6 billion years old. The oxygen was bound in water and metallic oxides on surface rocks and particles, and there was no oxygen in the free gaseous state. Furthermore, there was no ozone layer to absorb the sun's ultraviolet rays, which would harm or even kill animal life. Lifeless chemicals, in the absence of oxygen, were transformed into the living matter over one billion years. [8]

The early gas cloud was rich in hydrogen. The hydrogen of the primordial earth chemically united with carbon to form methane, nitrogen to form ammonia, and oxygen to form water vapour. The early atmosphere contained hydrogen, methane, ammonia, and water primarily. The water vapour in the atmosphere condensed into drops and fell as rain. The rain eroded the rocks and washed minerals into the sea, and this set the scene for the combination of the various chemical elements. Chemicals from the atmosphere mixed and reacted with those in the water to form a range of hydrocarbons (compounds made of hydrogen and carbon). Amino acids (made from water, hydrocarbons, and ammonia) are the building blocks for larger proteins. In the primitive seas, amino acids built up in large quantities and linked together to form proteins. Proteins are termed "organic" because living organisms make them. Organic compounds are synthesised from simple molecules by the energy of sunlight. But how were amino acids synthesised on the primitive Earth? On the primitive Earth, ultraviolet rays from the sun, electrical discharges, for example, lightning, and intense dry heat from volcanic activities, provided the energy to join the simple carbon compounds and nitrogenous substances into amino acids. On the primitive earth, proteins were produced randomly, but life did not begin with a self-sustaining network of proteins that could not be self-replicated. However, self-replicating nucleic acids such as ribonucleic acid (RNA) can be self-replicated and were present before proteins were synthesised. Once RNA appeared in the primitive seas, deoxyribonucleic acid (DNA) followed. DNA has a double helix structure and is the repository of genetic information. RNA molecules continue to direct protein synthesis. So, in modern cells, genetic information is stored in DNA, copied into RNA, and translated into protein. The richness of life comes from the endless permutation of nucleic acids into proteins. [8]

Origin and evolution of humankind on earth – When the true origin of humanity is discussed, the religious community and Bible believers find it offensive and unacceptable to think that we might have evolved from apes who lived millions of years ago. They are adamant about adhering to Genesis' creation account, which provides a chronological order in which God created the world without specifying how He did it. It is truly amazing that modern humans with impressive and wide-ranging characteristics and abilities, such as musicality, artistic talent, technical know-how, and intense religious and personal emotions, have evolved from primitive apes. When the complexities of evolution are considered, they indicate a highly creative process. Nothing can be created out of thin air, not even by God. Hence, Genesis should not be taken literally because it yields no useful information about the events and processes that brought humankind into existence. It is time to turn the marvels of scientific knowledge into a more helpful tool to understand the splendours of God's creation. Darwin's theory of evolution and the evidence gathered from fossil discoveries provide a more convincing explanation of the origin of humanity, with enormous implications for the biblical account of creation.

A time-line of human evolution - The closest relatives of humankind are the apes. The line leading to humans diverged from the ape branch. The evolutionary process produced a family of human ancestors in much the same way other groups of organisms became highly diversified. There were coexisting species of human ancestors throughout most of the evolutionary past, leading to homo sapiens. After a gap of a few million years, the first Hominid appeared about 4 million years ago. The hominid is a primate of a family known as Hominidae, including humans. Members of humankind are known as homo. Homo evolved in Africa about 2.5 million years ago. The more advanced and more humanlike species of hominid is called Homo habilis. Homo habilis was able to make stone tools, hence the specific name habilis, which means handy. This was a primitive human and was evolving alongside the less hominized species. The early hominids were mainly gatherers of plants and small animal life and used tools for digging, processing plant foods, scavenging meat into chewable pieces, and smashing large bones to get at the fat-rich bone marrow. Male and females exploited food resources, promoting food sharing, a major social engagement unique to humans. Homo habilis did not migrate beyond Africa, lasted for 500,000 years, and then became extinct. Homo erectus followed the extinction of homo habilis and appeared on the scene about 1.3 million to 300,000 years ago. Homo erectus were toolmakers and hunters who had learned to control fire because of a larger brain size than the species that went extinct before them. Moreover, Homo erectus were travellers and explorers that migrated from Africa to Asia and Europe. Homo erectus became extinct 27,000 to 53,000 years ago. When the Homo erectus existed, Homo Neanderthals and Homo sapiens were also roaming the earth. All the evidence suggests that more than one hominid species could have existed at any time in the past. There is no clear indication of how Homo erectus evolved into Homo sapiens, but it is estimated that Homo sapiens evolved about 300,000 years ago. The Neanderthals evolved at least 230,000 to 30,000 years ago, made complex stone tools and hunted large animals, cared for their sick and infirmed, buried their dead with various ritual objects, and lived mainly in Europe. The Neanderthals were replaced with Homo sapiens (modern humans) about 40,000 years ago, but the fossil evidence suggests that the Neanderthals and modern humans coexisted for 10,000 years. However, DNA studies have shown that the Neanderthals made a small contribution to the genes of modern humans. [8]

There is no consensus as to how Homo sapiens populated the globe. Modern humans may have evolved in Africa between 150,000 and 100,000 years ago and migrated to various regions of the globe. Subsequently, regional variations emerged in different geographical populations. Some researchers believe that modern human populations are descended from distinct ancient hominid lineages evolving independently of one another. Africa is the continent from which Homo erectus and Homo sapiens migrated some 1000,000 and 150,000 years ago, respectively. [8]

Human societies and emergence of families - One of the significant events in the Homo erectus period was the evolution of human society. Homo erectus were hunters by nature. Males hunted, whereas females did not participate in hunting and cared for the young. This organisation helped to strengthen mother-child bonds and, at the same time, reduced the mother's mobility. Eventually, there was a limitation on the male in the number of females he could support, and the monogamous structure took root. The monogamous structure caused a more permanent bonding between males and females and reduced sexual competition among the males. The prolonged male-female cohabitation increased the likelihood of leaving descendants. The family unit became more stable, and permanent shelters for gathering, rest, and play became more common. Human language started to develop, and females recorded and transmitted information to each other, children, and their male partners. Language's significant benefit was enhancing cooperation between groups, communities, and geographical areas. Closer corporations brought an exchange of ideas and began human cultural development. This critical period of human evolution created a blueprint for the society in which we live today. [8]

Summary – The closest relatives of humankind are the apes. The more advanced and human-like species of hominid is called Homo habilis. Homo erectus followed the extinction of Homo habilis. At the time Homo erectus existed, Homo Neanderthals and Homo sapiens were present on earth too. The Neanderthals were replaced by Homo sapiens (modern humans). Modern humans may have evolved in Africa and migrated to various regions of the globe. Then, regional variations emerged in different geographical populations. Modern human geographical populations are descended from different ancient hominid lineages, evolving independently of one another. [8]

Chapter 5
A scientific/biblical view of the origin of God and creation of humankind

The scientific and technological advances made in the last two centuries since the Western European Enlightenment are truly remarkable. Never in the recent history of humanity has so much knowledge been accumulated. However, this incredible scientific progress has not contributed to faith in God, and in most cases, it has challenged the existence of God. Science does not in itself prove or disprove creation and a creator. Sceptical and hostile atheists use scientific knowledge to their advantage. A view of the origin of God and humankind that utilises both science and biblical revelation can provide an exciting narrative. Whenever an attempt is made, the question of the origin of God and the exact processes that created the universe and life on earth may remain a mystery and a subject of interest and speculation for generations to come.

Science is based on empirical observations and the use of mathematics. It is a highly effective method for studying the laws of nature. However, science does not prove or disprove the existence of God, and it is left to the faithful and Bible believers to use the incredible pool of scientific knowledge to speculate on the origin of God and the wonders of His creation. Even though the great scientific advances in recent years have broadened our human horizons and understanding of the universe and life on earth, we can only speculate. The author expresses a view on the origin of God and the creation of humankind using scientific knowledge and the verses in Genesis, as well as information from the Gospels that are not included in the Bible.

Biblical/scientific origin of God – Quantum fluctuations occur when there is an unexpected change in the amount of energy at a point in space. [2,9] There might have been countless quantum fluctuations occurring randomly in space, and one unique event might have produced a being of light whom we have come to know as God. But can this be possible? According to Jesus, the light, our living father, was not created but came into existence of its own accord and had a beginning. (Thomas 50) But where did the light come into existence from? Could it be from a random change in the amount of energy in a point in space (a quantum event)? The light could only have come into existence from darkness since light can never create darkness. Hence, the space where quantum fluctuations occur is darkness. As mentioned, science tells us that about 99% of the universe is made of dark energy or dark matter. [2] Light and darkness co-existed in the same place, and the light could not stay with the darkness forever. Since light can't destroy darkness, it devised a method to free itself from coexisting with darkness in the same place. [6] Light created man in His image; in the image of God, He created him. He created a male and a female. (Genesis 1:27) The creation of humankind was aimed at ending the co-existence of light and darkness, and the redemption of humanity became the centrepiece of God's providence and work. [6] But before humanity could appear on earth, other forms of life, such as plants and animals, had to be created. How did God create life on earth?

Origin of life on earth – As mentioned in Chapter 1, the universe cooled down from extremely high temperatures after the Big Bang, and the celestial bodies and planets, including the earth, were formed. [2] The earth was a lifeless, empty rock in space, and God changed it into an oasis of life. How did God do it? Jesus said, "Listen, a sower came forth, took a handful, and cast. Now, some fell upon the path, and the birds came and picked them out. Others fell upon a rock and did not take root in the soil and did not send up ears. And others fell upon thorns, and they choked the seed, and the grubs devoured them. And others fell upon good soil, and it sent up good crops and yielded sixty per measure and a hundred and twenty per measure." [5] (Thomas 9). God resembles a gardener who puts seeds into the soil to produce a harvest. A good harvest requires seeds, soil, and water. The soil was the planet earth, which was void at the beginning. So, God (the gardener) covered its surface with oceans of liquid water produced by hydrogen inside the earth and delivered to the earth by impact from icy celestial bodies. [10] When liquid water is present, the earth becomes fertile land for life to emerge. But where did the seed come from? Usually, a gardener takes a seed from a seed bank and plants it into the soil. It is likely that God is a seed-maker and made a seed to produce various forms of life, including humankind. The seed contained the basic genetic codes of all the living beings, and when the seed was planted in the soil of the earth, it died, and a tree of life in all its complexities and wonders appeared on earth. Is this feasible? Jesus said, "The harvest is plentiful, but the workers are few. So, plead with the lord to dispatch workers for the harvest." [5] (Thomas 73). In this parable, God is the gardener who planted the seed of humanity. The seed died and produced various life forms, including human beings who must be harvested.

Consider a gardener who puts an apple seed into the soil and waters it until the seed dies and becomes a fully-grown tree. The tree produces apples. Some apples are good, and some are bad. Once the harvest is ready, the gardener picks the apples, keeps the good ones, and throws away the bad ones. A gardener can never create apples spontaneously; the tree does it over time at its own pace, and God can never create humans instantly out of thin air. As Jesus said, "light, of its own accord alone, came into existence and stood at rest." [5] Life forms, including humankind, come into existence of their own accords and can never be created suddenly out of nothing, a universal law that is consistent with Darwin's evolution by natural selection. Therefore, Darwin's claim that life requires a very long time to develop into its final form is credible. In the book of Enoch, the account of the creation of humankind is somewhat different.

God created all things living, and then he created man. He created a man and a woman and gave them dominion over all things. God named the man Adam and the woman; He named Lilith. Both were created from earth's dust, and both received the breath of life from God. They became human souls, and God endowed them with the power of speech. Created at the same time, in the same way, there was no master, no leader, and only bickering between them. Lilith said, "I will not be below you, in life or during sex. I want the superior position." But Adam would not relent and insisted that God had created him to be the head of the family and in the affairs of the earth. Lilith was enraged and would not submit. Lilith became frustrated, and in anger, she pronounced God's holy and ineffable name. Having corrupted the power of the name, she flew into the air, changing form, and disappeared out of sight, becoming demonic. God cursed Lilith, and her form was that of a succubus. God said, "It is not good for man to be alone." And the Lord God caused a deep sleep to fall on him, and he slept; and He took from Adam a rib from among his ribs for the woman, and this rib was the origin of the woman. And

He built up the flesh in its place and created the woman. [11] When God created Lilith from the dust of the earth, it was a disaster. She was imperfect and became rebellious, sinful, and cursed by God. God then used Adam's genetic material, or DNA, and modified it to create a woman, whom He called Eve. Even Eve was not perfect and disobeyed God's command and became sinful. [11] How can God not create a perfect being? The universal law does not permit perfect creation spontaneously. Everything that exists, be it God, celestial bodies, or living organisms, must come into existence of its own accord and should not be created instantly in its final form from dust and pre-existing genetic material. If the universal law is violated, it will have severe consequences for the created beings, like Lilith, who became a demon, and Eve, who became sinful. So, the rapid creation of organisms is against the universal law revealed by Jesus in Thomas 50. Recall that the earliest fossil evidence of life on earth dates to 3.7 billion years ago. There is no instantaneity in the workings of nature. [4,8,12] In the Bible, there is an account of creation that is different from the scientific model. The verses in Genesis in the Bible demonstrate the chronological order in which the world was made, and they should not be taken literally. For example, in verses 1:1-5, God created the heavens and the earth; and the earth being without form and empty, and darkness on the face of the deep, and the Spirit of God moving gently on the face of the waters, then God said, "Let light be – and there was. And God saw the light that it was good, and God separated between the light and darkness. And God called the light "Day." And He called the darkness "Night." And there was evening, and there was morning on the first day." Note that God separated the light and darkness, implying that light and darkness pre-existed the creation of the world and were not made by God.

The origin of life goes back almost three billion years ago to a "primordial soup". [2,8,12] The primordial soup is the seed that God placed on earth. Mysteriously, it had the genetic codes of all the living beings. The seed died and produced a tree from which life in its most vivid forms has come. The Darwinian theory of evolution by natural selection is, for now, probably the best explanation of the origin and development of life on earth. This is consistent with the universal law (Thomas 50) that says everything comes into existence of its own accord and reaches its final form. Recall that light, of its own accord, came into existence and gained its final form, a God as a being like humans. [5] Hence, the account of creation in Genesis 1:1-26 in the Bible must not be taken factually.

We can now formulate an idea about the origin of God and the creation of humanity based on scientific knowledge, Jesus's sayings in the Gospels of Philip and Thomas, and the Bible.

- Light (God) came into existence because of quantum fluctuations in space. Light and darkness co-existed in the same place in a state of duality. So, light devised a plan to free itself from the shadow of darkness. The goal was to create a humanity in whom the duality of light and darkness would be resolved for perpetuity, the plan for redemption.

- Light created the universe in a Big Bang, and as the universe cooled down, matter formed to make the celestial bodies and planets, including the earth.

- Once the earth was in place and water covered the surface, God made a seed (primordial soup) and planted it in the earth's soil. The seed died and produced the tree of life, from which all the living beings, including humankind, come. When humanity reached maturity, God's plan for redemption began. This will be discussed in the next chapter.

Summary – The scientific account of the origin of light (God) and the one recorded in the Gospel of Thomas are consistent. However, there are significant differences between the biblical and scientific accounts of the creation of the universe and humankind. The biblical account implies instantaneous creation, whereas the scientific model relies on an extended period for life to emerge from its primitive to its most complex and complete form, often through a harsh and ruthless struggle for existence.

Chapter 6
The greatest mystery of all – Faith, redemption, and the kingdom of light

The natural world's complexity, beauty, and wonders have captivated the human mind and imagination for millennia. However, behind the marvels of the natural world lies the mystery of faith. Mortal man rejects idolatry and immorality and seeks after an invisible God in his inner heart. Faith and obedience to God's moral law bring blessings and the promise of eternal life. When the blessings of God come through in the person of Jesus Christ, our imperfect mortality changes into the perfect immortality termed redemption. Then, the mystery of life and human existence is made known to the redeemed. Natural beauty is the shadow of man's redemption in Christ. But when the redemption is accomplished, the shadow disappears, and the light shines in its full glory and meaning forever, the start of eternity.

A universe with a purpose – Science teaches us that modern humans have evolved from primitive apes. If this is the case, faith in an invisible, living God is the greatest mystery of all, and the name of the patriarch Abraham is forever allied with it. As he was known at birth, Abram understood the errors of the earth that all went astray after graven images and uncleanness. His father worshipped idols, but Abram refused to follow in his father's footsteps and do the same thing. He began to pray to the Creator of all things that He might spare him from the errors of the children of men. Abram asked his father, "What help and profit have we from those idols which you worship, and in the presence of which you bow yourself? There is no spirit in them. They are dumb forms, and they mislead the heart. Do not worship them; Worship the God of heaven, who causes the rain and the dew to fall on the earth and does everything on the earth, and has created everything by His word, and all life is from His presence." And a word came into his heart, and he said, "All the signs of the stars, and the signs of the moon, and the sun are all in the hand of the Lord. Why do I search them out? If He desires, He causes it to rain, morning and evening, and if He desires, He withholds it, and all things are in his hand." He prayed in the night and said, "My God, God Most High, You alone are my God, and You and your dominion have I chosen." For the first time, a mortal sought after an invisible God from his inner heart. "And you have created all things, and all things that are the work of Your hands. Deliver me from the hands of evil spirits who have dominion over the thoughts of men's hearts, and let them not lead me astray from You, my God. And establish me and my offspring forever so that we do not go astray from now and forever." Then the word of the Lord was sent to him through an angel, saying, "Get out of your country, and from your kindred, and from the house of your father, and go to a land which I will show you, and I shall make you a great and numerous nation. And I will bless you, and I will make your name great, and you will be blessed, and I will bless those that bless you, and curse those that curse you. I will be a God to you and your son, and to your son's son, and to all your offspring, fear not, from now on and to all generations of the earth, I am your God." God changed Abram's name to Abraham. [11] How can it be that a mortal man rejects idolatry and immorality and seeks good conduct and faith in a single invisible deity from his inner heart? This is the greatest mystery of all and is the purpose for which the universe was created. At last, the tree of humanity, which was growing for about 1.8 billion years, produced fruit. Recall the parable of the gardener and the seed by Jesus? (Thomas 73) God planted the seed of life on earth and waited patiently; the seed died and became a tree;

the tree bore good and bad fruits. The gardener was delighted with the good fruit and rejected the bad ones. Abraham was the good fruit of the tree of humankind.

Abraham married Sarah and had a son, Isaac, with whom God made a covenant. Isaac married and had a son, Jacob, who wrestled with God. God changed Jacob's name to Israel because he persevered with God and with men and was able. (Genesis 32: 26-28) The descendants of Jacob are known as Israelites. God made a covenant with Israelites and gave them the ten commandments or moral law through His prophet Moses and his brother Aaron. God gave laws about Altars, the treatment of slaves, violent acts, repayment for stolen goods, justice and fairness, and various other religious laws. (Exodus 19-23) The idea was to make the children of Israel a model nation or a priesthood to serve God for the redemption of humanity. For this to succeed, Israel had to become strictly monotheistic in its belief and conduct and depend entirely on God for its subsistence and existence. Strict monotheism means unconditional faithfulness to God and strict obedience to His moral law for the covenant to bear fruit. God sanctified them, gathered them from among all the children of men, and commanded them to observe the sign of His covenant for their generations as eternal law. [11] But as time passed, the Israelites reverted to idolatry and immorality, displeasing God. Despite repeated warnings, the behaviour of the children of Israel resembled that of the pagan and godless ways of their ancestors and the gentile nations around them and became lawless and rebellious. God expressed His anger frequently. "Have you not now called to Me: My father, You are the friend of my youth? Will He keep His anger forever? Or will He guard it to the end? Behold, you have spoken, and you have done all the evil things that you could". (Jeremiah 3: 4-5) God's repeated calls to repentance were unheeded. "If you will return, O Israel, says Jehovah, return to Me. And if you will put away your hateful idols out of My face, and will not waver, and you will swear, As Jehovah lives, in truth, in justice, and in righteousness; even the nations shall bless themselves in Him, and in Him, they will glorify. (Jeremiah 4: 1-3) "So says Jehovah, "Stand by the ways and see; and ask for then old paths where the good way is and walk in it, and you shall find rest for your souls." But they said. "We will not walk in it." "So hear, O nations; and know, O congregation, that which is coming on them. Hear, O earth; behold, I will bring evil on this people, the fruit of their thoughts. For they have not listened to My words, and My law, they also rejected it." (Jeremiah 6:16-19) Israelites never became monotheists, and the covenant failed. Humankind's instinct is to worship pagan gods and offer blood sacrifices in temples dedicated to idols. The Holy God commanded the Israelites to put their trust in Him and obey His moral laws unreservedly. But how can enforced monotheism and command to follow rigid external moral law remedy ignorance, ungodliness, apathy, and vanity in the heart of sinful humans? [13] The problem of idolatry and immorality lies in the heart of sinful humans, and nothing less than a fundamental change will remedy the problem. God promised to transform the heart of the Israelites to make them obedient and faithful to His moral law. "Behold the days come, says Jehovah, that I will cut a new covenant with the house of Israel, and with the house of Judah, not according to the covenant that I cut with their fathers in the day I took them by the hand to bring them out of the land of Egypt – Which covenant of Mine they broke, although I was a husband to them, says Jehovah – but this shall be the covenant that I will cut with the house of Israel: After those days, declares Jehovah, I will put my law in their inward parts, and I will write it on their hearts, and I will be their God, and they shall be My people. And they shall no longer teach his neighbour, and each man his brother, saying, Know Jehovah. For they shall all know Me, from the least of them even to the greatest of them, declares Jehovah. For I will forgive their iniquity, and I will remember their sins no more." (Jeremiah 31: 31-34) The remedy came in the form of the person of Jesus Christ. Mary, Jesus's mother, was engaged to Joseph, but Jesus was conceived without Mary and Joseph having a relationship, a virgin birth. (Matt 1:18) Jesus was born in Judea and raised in the Jewish tradition. After Jesus was baptised by John the Baptist, he started his work in Galilee. Jesus's teaching and healing acts are scattered throughout the New Testament of the Bible. Jesus healed blinds, lame men, lepers, physically and mentally disabled, sick men and women, demon-possessed men, and paralysed men. Light (God) was in Jesus Christ, redeeming humanity. In Christ, the duality of light and darkness was resolved forever, and the light is no longer under the shadow of darkness. The God (light) in Jesus Christ expresses Himself in clear terms. "I am the living bread that came down from Heaven. If anyone eats of this bread, he will live forever. And indeed, the bread which

I will give is My flesh, which I will give for the life of the world." (John 6:51) "I am the True Vine, and My Father is the Vine-dresser. Every branch in Me not bearing fruit, He takes it away; and each one bearing fruit, He prunes so that it may bear more fruit. You are already pruned because of the word which I have spoken to you. Remain in Me, and I in you. As the branch is not able to bear fruit of itself, unless it remains in the vine, so neither can you unless you remain in Me." (John 12:1-5) "While I am in the world, I am the light of the world." (John 9: 5) "I am the good shepherd, and I know those that are Mine; and I am known by the ones that are Mine." (John 10:14) "I am the Way, the Truth, and the Life. No one comes to the Father except through Me. If you had known Me, you would have known My Father also; from now on, you do know Him and have seen Him." (John 14:6) "I am the door. If anyone enters through Me, he will be saved, and will go in, and will go out, and will find pasture." (John 10:9) "I am the resurrection and the Life; the one believing into Me, though he dies, he shall live." (John 11:25)

Two events in the life of Jesus are important. His ministry in Galilee and His travel to Jerusalem. In his sermon, Jesus blessed the poor, the meek, the merciful, the peacemakers, and those who mourn, hunger, are pure in heart, and persecuted for righteousness. (Matt 5: 3-11) The greatest commandments are: "You shall love the Lord your God with all your heart, and with all your soul, and with all your strength, and with all your mind; and your neighbour as yourself." (Luke 10: 27) Jesus travelled to the Jewish temple in Jerusalem and made a prophecy of its coming end. And going out, Jesus left the temple. And his disciples came to show him the building of the temple. But Jesus said to them, "Do you not see all these things?" Truly I say to you, "There will not at all be left one stone on a stone which in no way will not be thrown down." (Matt 24: 1-2) As Jesus predicted, the Roman armies destroyed the temple in 70 AD, bringing the Jewish presence in Palestine to an end. In 1946 the land was again re-populated with Jewish refugees and migrants from Europe and far beyond, creating the secular Zionist state of Israel in the Middle East. There is a plan to build a third temple in Jerusalem where according to the biblical prophecies, the man of sin shall sit in the temple and blasphemy the name of the Holy God. "But when you see the abomination of desolation, the one spoken of by Daniel the prophet, standing where it ought not – he reading, let him understand – then let those in Judea flee into the mountains." (Mark 13:14) After the final judgement, the new heaven and earth will come for the redeemed in Jesus Christ, and a new age will begin when light and darkness are divided forever. The light will preside over the kingdom of the redeemed, and darkness will rule over the dominion of hell and the damned. The purpose for which the universe was created will be fulfilled when eternity comes. But for now, "The harvest truly is great, but the workers few. Pray then that the Lord of the harvest may send out workers into His harvest." (Matt 9: 37)

Miracles in the Bible – A miracle is an extraordinary event that is not explainable by the laws of science. There are records of miracles performed by God, prophets, and Jesus throughout the Bible. Here are a few. When Moses threw a stick down on the ground, it turned into a snake. (Exodus 4:3) God commanded Moses, "Raise your staff, and stretch out your hand over the sea, and divide it so that the sons of Israel may go in the midst of the sea on dry ground." (Exodus 14:16) Jehovah said to Moses, "Behold, I Am." Bread will rain from the heavens for you. (Exodus 16:4) Jesus and his disciples attended a marriage in Galilee and changed water into the vine. (John 2:1-11) Labouring all through the night, Simon took no fish. But at Your word, I will let down the net, said Simon. Jesus gave the word and Simon netted a great multitude of fish, and their net was being torn. (Luke 5:6) When Jesus was with his disciples in the boat, a great storm rose up in the sea. His disciples awakened him, saying, Lord, save us. We are perishing. Then rising up, Jesus rebuked the winds and the sea. And there was a great calm. (Matt 8:23-27)

How can science explain the miracles in the Bible? According to Einstein's equation, energy, E; mass, m; and speed of light, c; are related by $E = mc^2$. [14] Light, mass, and energy are interchangeable. One good example is a nuclear explosion. Using Einstein's equation, an atomic bomb is detonated when a small amount of the matter is changed into a tremendous amount of energy and light through nuclear fission. [14,15] The natural and physical laws do not permit intervention, but God is light and lives and has all His creative power in the quantum domain. The natural world emerged from a quantum beginning, and its laws can be changed by light (God), who lives in the quantum domain. One may say that $E = mc^2$ is where God lives and performs all His creative work. The quantum dominion has precedence over the natural world and can overrule its laws instantly. At the opening of the Red Sea, the water, m, was changed into energy, E, at the speed of light, creating the dry ground. Similarly, water was transformed into the vine at the quantum level spontaneously. Humans cannot duplicate the miracles in the Bible because they live in the natural world where no intervention is allowed, but there are no limitations for God, who lives in the quantum domain.

Summary - Empirical science carefully considers hypothesis, theory, or observation. It designs, executes experiments, and analyses the results in detail, often supported by mathematics. It tells us that the universe, celestial bodies, and life on earth resulted from a random Big Bang event in the distant past. That life evolved over millions of years through the struggle for existence by natural selection and has no purpose. In contrast, the book of Genesis is a chronological account of the creation of the universe and life on earth with a stated purpose: to redeem humanity through the person of Jesus Christ. Neither science nor religion can ever answer all the questions about human existence, but a more thought-provoking picture emerges when they are considered together.

Chapter 7
Summary and conclusions

The laws of science do not permit intervention by a supernatural being. The quantum domain where God exists has precedence over the natural and physical laws, enabling God to intervene in the created order whenever He chooses. All living and inanimate things come into existence of their own accord and gain their final forms from a simple and primitive beginning like a seed or a primordial soup. God can never spontaneously create anything out of thin air and out of nothing. The body of Christ is Israel's abode, where those whom God calls to serve Him are redeemed. Once the redemption of the elect is completed, the bride will be ready to meet her bridegroom at the second coming of Christ.

- Science unlocks the laws of the natural world, and religion does those of the spiritual realm. Science tells us that the strict laws of physics and biology govern the working of the natural world. Violating these laws will lead to disaster and destruction. Religion teaches us that human conduct must always depend on God's moral law, and a departure from it will have serious consequences. Despite fundamental differences between science and religion, the message is clear. These laws seem inter connected, and whenever they are broken, calamity ensues. As the history of humanity shows, cataclysms have always overshadowed human existence and experience since the dawn of time. Perhaps the chaos unfolding in the natural world reflects humanity's poor spiritual condition. Redemption is in the person of Jesus Christ, and humanity finds its peace only in him. It is time to embrace the message of the Gospel of Christ: "Come to Me, all those labouring and being burdened, and I will give you rest." (Matt 11:28)

- We do well to remember what Jesus said. "It is from the light that we have come – from the place where light, of its own accord alone, came into existence and stood at rest." All living and inanimate things come into existence by their own accords and gain their final forms from a simple and primitive beginning like a seed or a primordial soup. God can never spontaneously create anything out of thin air and out of nothing. Like a gardener, God puts a seed into the soil to die, and after the seed dies, it produces a tree, and the tree bears fruit after exposure to the harsh and punishing weathering conditions over time. God then harvests the fruit, choosing the good and rejecting the bad ones. God is seed-maker par excellence. Jesus is the perfect man, but before perfection was made incarnate, an imperfect mortal (Abraham) had to evolve from its primitive form. The great wonders of the universe and the natural world have a humble beginning.

- Whatever happened to God's plan after the covenant with the Israelites failed? Jesus was with his twelve apostles. And taking a loaf, giving thanks, He broke it and gave it to them, saying, "This is My body being given for you. Do this for My remembrance." In the same way, the cup also, after having supped, saying, "This cup is the New Covenant in My blood, which is being poured out for you." (Luke 22:19-20) The covenant was revived in Christ. The body of Christ is made up of individuals who are called to serve him, and the blood, symbolising his spirit to cleanse his followers, is where the faithful Israel, or model nation, is being prepared before Jesus return. In the second coming, redeemed Israel through Christ will rule over the nations in the kingdom of God.

References

1. Maurice Ashley, The Golden Century, Europe 1598-1715, CARDINAL, Sphere Books Ltd, London, 1975 (ISBN 0 351 15152 4).

2. Lawrence M. Krauss, "a universe from nothing", Simon & Schuster, London, 2012   (ISBN: 978-1-47111-268-3).

3. https://www.thefreedictionary.com/quantum
   Date visited: 24-05-2022

4. Charles Darwin, "The origin of species", Avenel Books, New York, 1979   (ISBN: 0-517-30978-5)

5. Bentley Layton, "The Gnostic Scriptures", SCM Press Ltd, London, 1987.   (ISBN: 0-334-02022-0).

6. Ali Ansarifar, "Why did God create mankind?", The problem of duality with God., Balboa Press, UK, 2021 (IBSN: 978-1-9822-8439-8)

7. https://microspedia.blogspot.com/2020/07/picture-of-atom-through-electron.html   Date visited: 01-07-2022

8. E. Peter Volpe, Peter A. Rosenbaum, "Understanding evolution", McGraw Hill,
   London. (IBSN: 0-697-05137-4)

9. https://simple.wikipedia.org/wiki/Quantum_fluctuation Date visited:09-07-2022

10. https://en.wikipedia.org/wiki/Planetesimal Date visited: 16-06-2022

11. Joseph B. Lumpkin, "The Books of Enoch", The Angels, The Watchers and the Nephilim, Fifth Estate Publishers, 2011. (IBSN: 9781936533077)

12. https://www.scienceabc.com/pure-sciences/how-did-life-on-earth-begin.html Date visited: 06-06-2022

13. Ali Ansarifar, "The March to the Armageddon", Balboa Press UK, 2021. (ISBN: 978-1-9822-8377-3 (sc), ISBN: 978-1-9822-8378-0 (e)

14. Abraham Pais, "The science and the life of Albert Einstein", Oxford University Press, Oxford, 1982. (ISBN: 0-19-853907-X)

15. https://byjus.com/physics/what-is-nuclear-fission/ Date visited: 03-06-2022

All scripture quotations have been taken from The Interlinear Bible, Hebrew-Greek- English. Jay P. Green, Sr. Hendrickson Publishers, 2020. (ISBN: 978-1-56563-977-5) 8.

Epilogue

The Western European Enlightenment during the 17th and 18th centuries, referred to as the Age of Reason, significantly impacted our understanding of the universe and the development of life on earth. The invention of modern instruments such as microscopes, telescopes, and thermometers, and the rise of contemporary science, for example, physics and mathematics, enabled knowledge to be gained by rational and experimental methods, which paved the way for the scientific, philosophical, and political revolutions of the 18th and 19th centuries. The Enlightenment opposed the fixed dogmas of the church and religious orthodoxy and promoted individual liberty, religious tolerance, and the use of vigorous scientific methods and reductionism. As a result, the influence of the Catholic Church declined, and the religious laws of the day and the legal systems were reformed. The Enlightenment shaped other fields of intellectual endeavour, for instance, religion and history. During this period of intellectual awakening, the conflict between science and religion flared up and continues to this day. It is not always appreciated that science does not prove or disprove the existence of a deity. Still, atheists and disbelievers often use it to make a case against the existence of God and dismiss the credibility of biblical revelation. Scientific knowledge can be used to understand the Genesis of creation, producing a fascinating story to tell. Science tells us that life on earth has evolved from primitive to highly complex forms over millions of years. The struggle for existence by natural selection ensures that the fittest species survive to populate the earth, which also applies to the human species that have evolved from primitive apes. Bible believers may find this notion highly offensive and reject humanity's scientific origin, but this is a misguided sentiment. Once the scientific facts are considered in conjunction with the biblical account of human creation, a fascinating picture emerges of the mystery of life, with faith and redemption at its centre.

Afterword

I am a scientist by profession and a Christian. The conflict between science and religion has always puzzled me. Science is a very efficient method for generating knowledge about our universe. Since the age of enlightenment and scientific and industrial revolutions, humanity has benefitted massively from the discoveries and technological advances brought about by science. Science has created the modern industrial age that is unprecedented in human history. But, this has caused a serious conflict between man's religious beliefs in a supernatural God that goes back thousands of years and the modern scientific view of the world. The reason for this conflict is not fully understood since science is empirical and based on the observation of the natural world by human senses and physical instruments and requires proof.

In contrast, religion is metaphysical and relies heavily on personal conviction and faith; often, no proof is necessary or demanded. Once it is appreciated that science and religion are different in constitution, methods, and practice, then scientific knowledge can be used to understand the Genesis of human creation in the Bible. Genesis in the Bible states what steps God took to create the world but does not say how. Science provides answers in a way no other source of knowledge, theological, philosophical, and metaphysical, can ever do. It is time to make science friendlier to the holy scriptures and reap the benefits from its immense source of treasured knowledge.

Final remarks

We live in a most exciting period in human history, the age of science. The knowledge generated by scientific methods and instruments is amazing and highly beneficial to humanity. Therefore, it is best to leave sentimentality behind and use scientific knowledge to understand the biblical account of the creation of the universe and humankind. It will be to our detriment if we do not do so.

About the author

Dr. Ali Ansarifar has been living in the U.K. for over 40 years. He was awarded a bachelor's degree, a doctorate in Materials Science from Queen Mary College, the University of London, and a Diploma in Interface Science from Imperial College, University of London. He worked as a post-doctoral research assistant at Imperial College, London, and Cavendish Laboratory, Department of Physics of the University of Cambridge. He was an upper senior research scientist in a rubber research and development centre in Hertfordshire, U.K., and a lecturer in Polymer Engineering in the Materials Department at Loughborough University until he retired as a senior lecturer. He has given lectures, seminars and workshops in the United States, the United Kingdom, Europe, the Middle East and Southeast Asia, published over 150 technical research papers in peer-reviewed international scientific journals and technical magazines for the polymer and tire industries and textbooks, and contributed chapters to scientific books. He has been on the editorial board of rubber and adhesion scientific journals and has been awarded prizes for his scientific publications. He is a Fellow of the Higher Education Academy U.K. and a servant of Jesus Christ.

About the book

This book is written to address the conflict between science and religion. Since science is empirical and religion metaphysical, there can be no conflict between the two. The alleged conflict is caused when atheists and disbelievers use science and scientific knowledge to discredit the existence of a supernatural God, religious view of the universe, and the origin of humanity. It is acceptable to use the treasure chest of scientific knowledge to help understand the biblical account of the world's creation. Once this is achieved, the creation story becomes more exciting and accessible to modern humans.

The book reviews the cosmological model of the universe based on the Big Bang and the Darwinian theory of the struggle for existence by natural selection. The biblical and scientific views on the origin of humanity will be examined separately. Then, an idea on the origin of God and humankind will be proposed based on science and the biblical narrative. Faith is the greatest mystery of all, and redemption through the person of Jesus Christ is the reason for the universe's existence and the creation of humanity. In Genesis, light and darkness co-existed and were separated to create the world, but in the person of Jesus Christ, they are separated forever, and redemption is achieved. The apparent conflict between science and religion is replaced with more positive use of scientific knowledge to understand Genesis in the Bible.

Acknowledgement

The photograph of the author was produced by

ZigZag Photography, Leicester

UK studio@zigzagphotography.co.uk

www.ingramcontent.com/pod-product-compliance
Lightning Source LLC
Chambersburg PA
CBHW050303120526
44590CB00016B/2468